My First Quokka Book

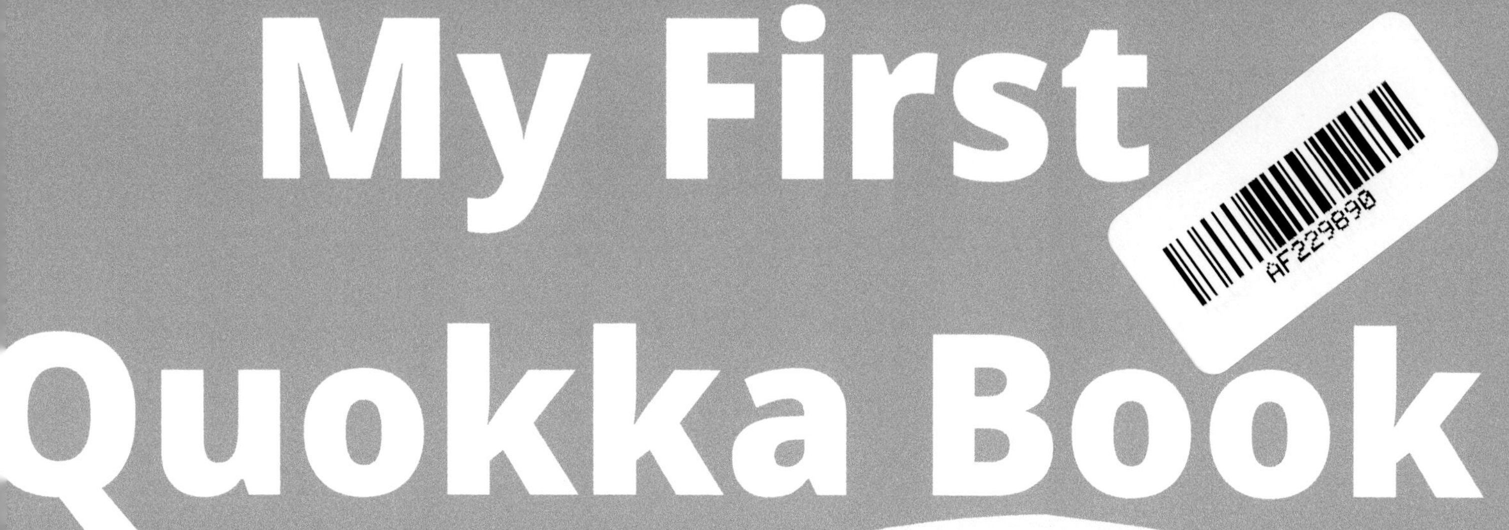

By Carrie Casey

This **STEM** book is designed to introduce children to a vulnerable marsuplial.

NEED CONTENT HERE

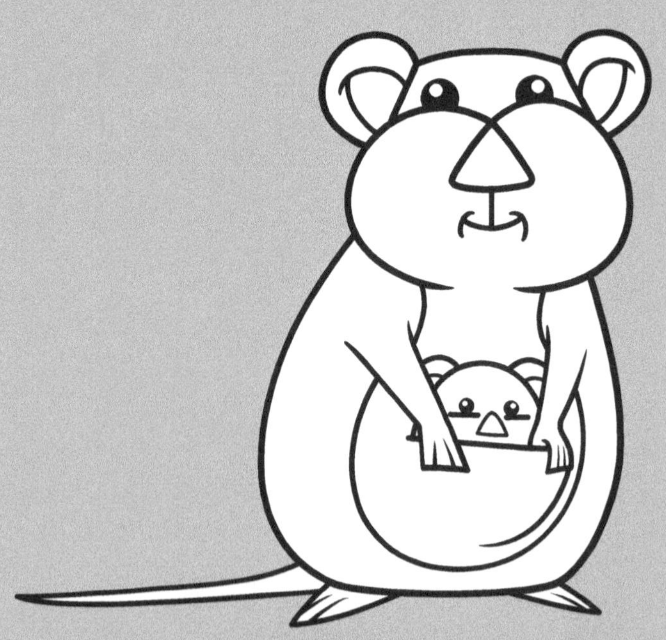

Published by CEY Press
821 Grand Ave, Suite 119
Pflugerville, TX 78660

ISBN: 978-1-954885-24-0

I

My First Quokka Book

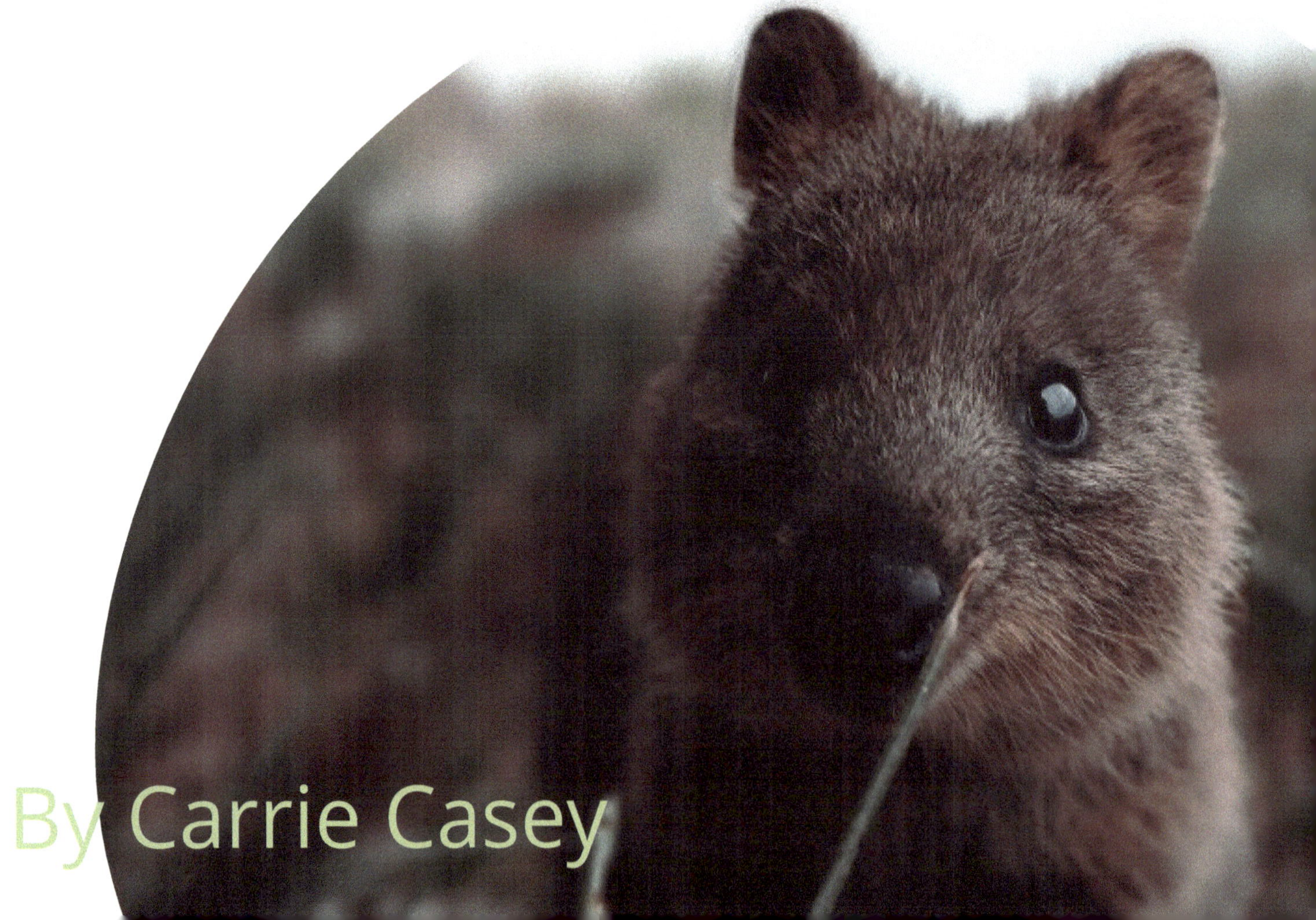

By Carrie Casey

Meet the Quokka. The happiest animal on earth.

pronounced /ˈkwäkə/ or /kwok-uh /

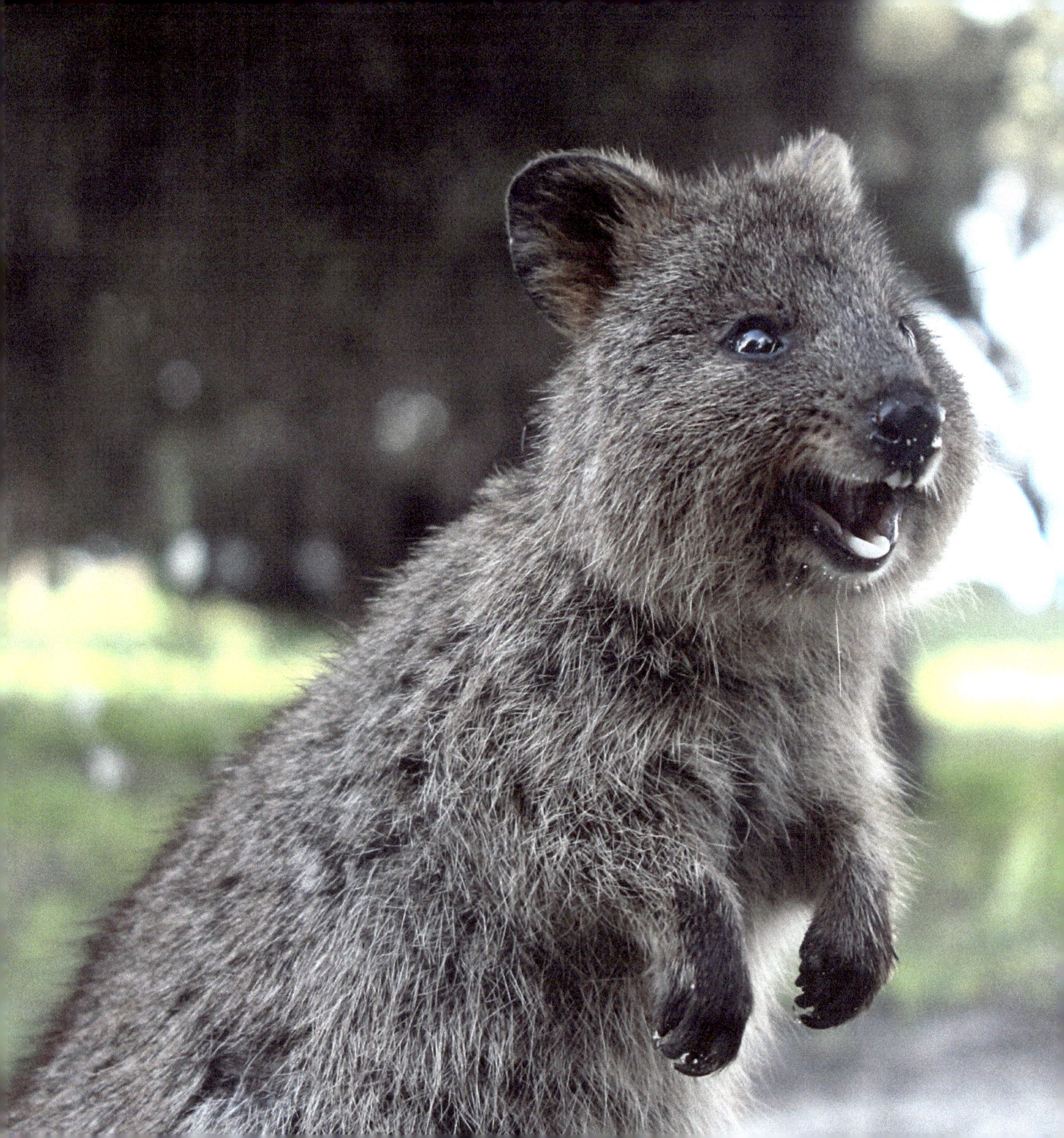

Isn't that a funny name?

QU0OOO KA

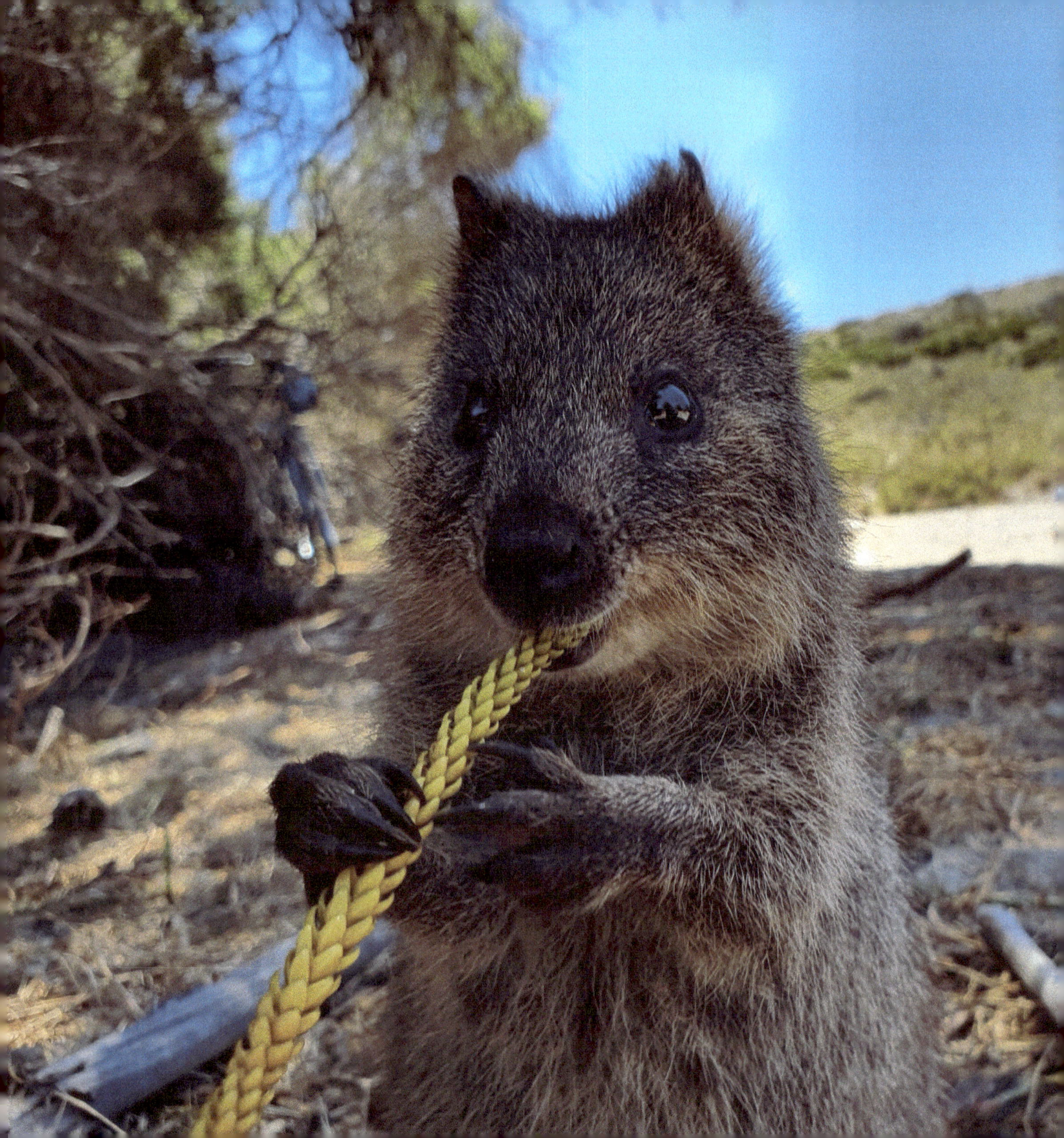

They are small,
friendly
Australian animals.

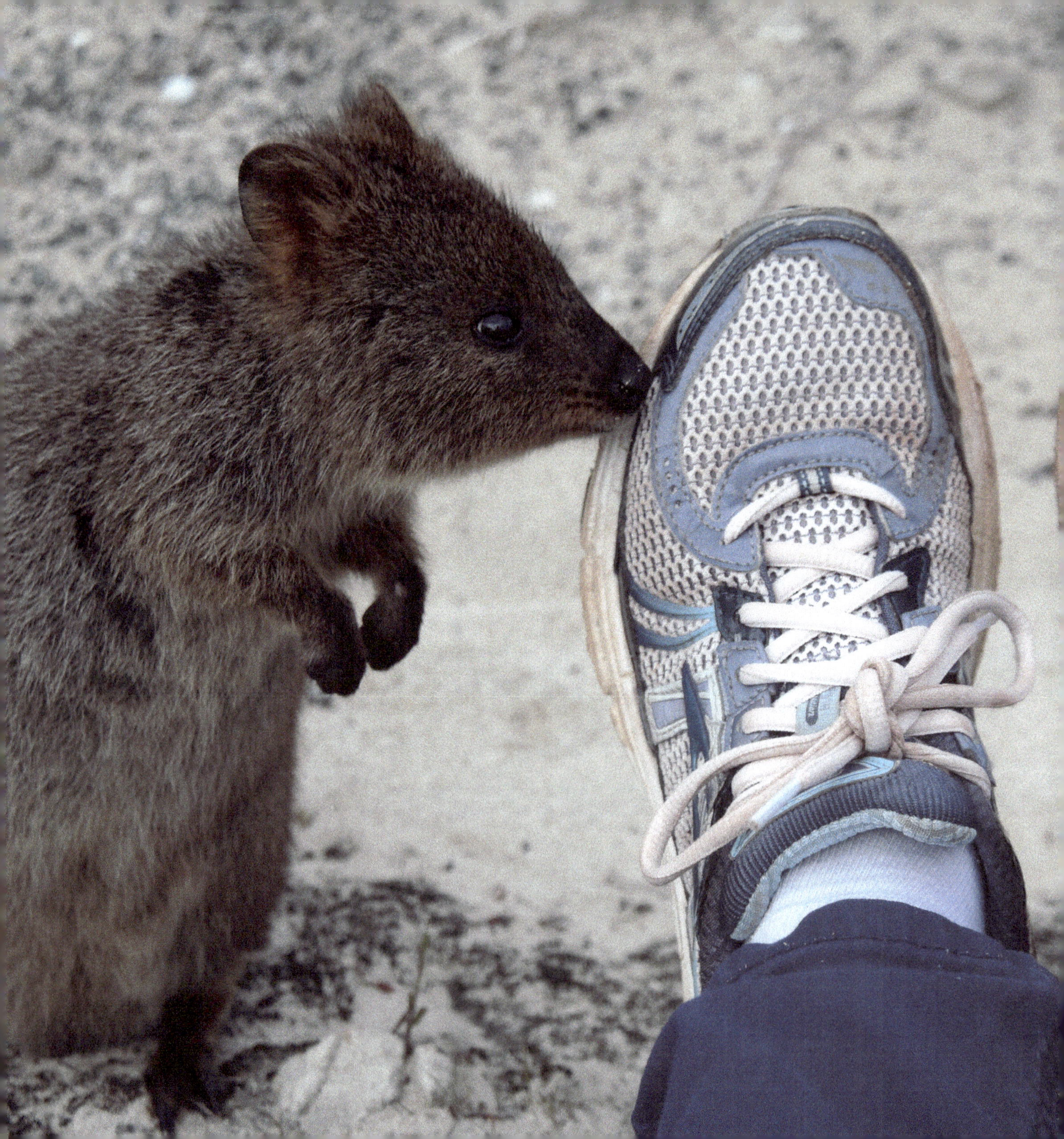

When most people think about Australia, think about Kangaroos.

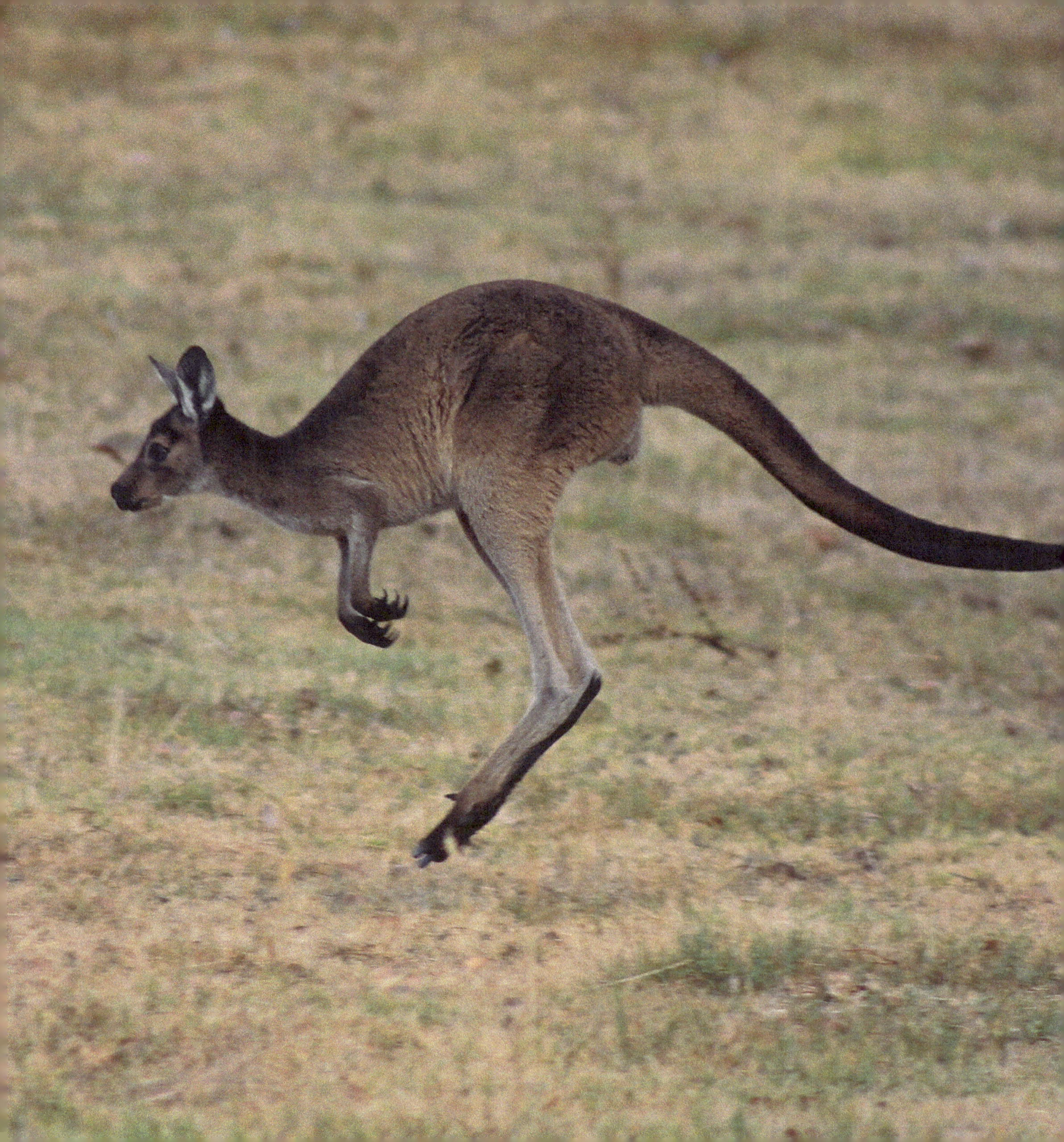

Kangaroos are Quokka's bigger, more famous cousins.

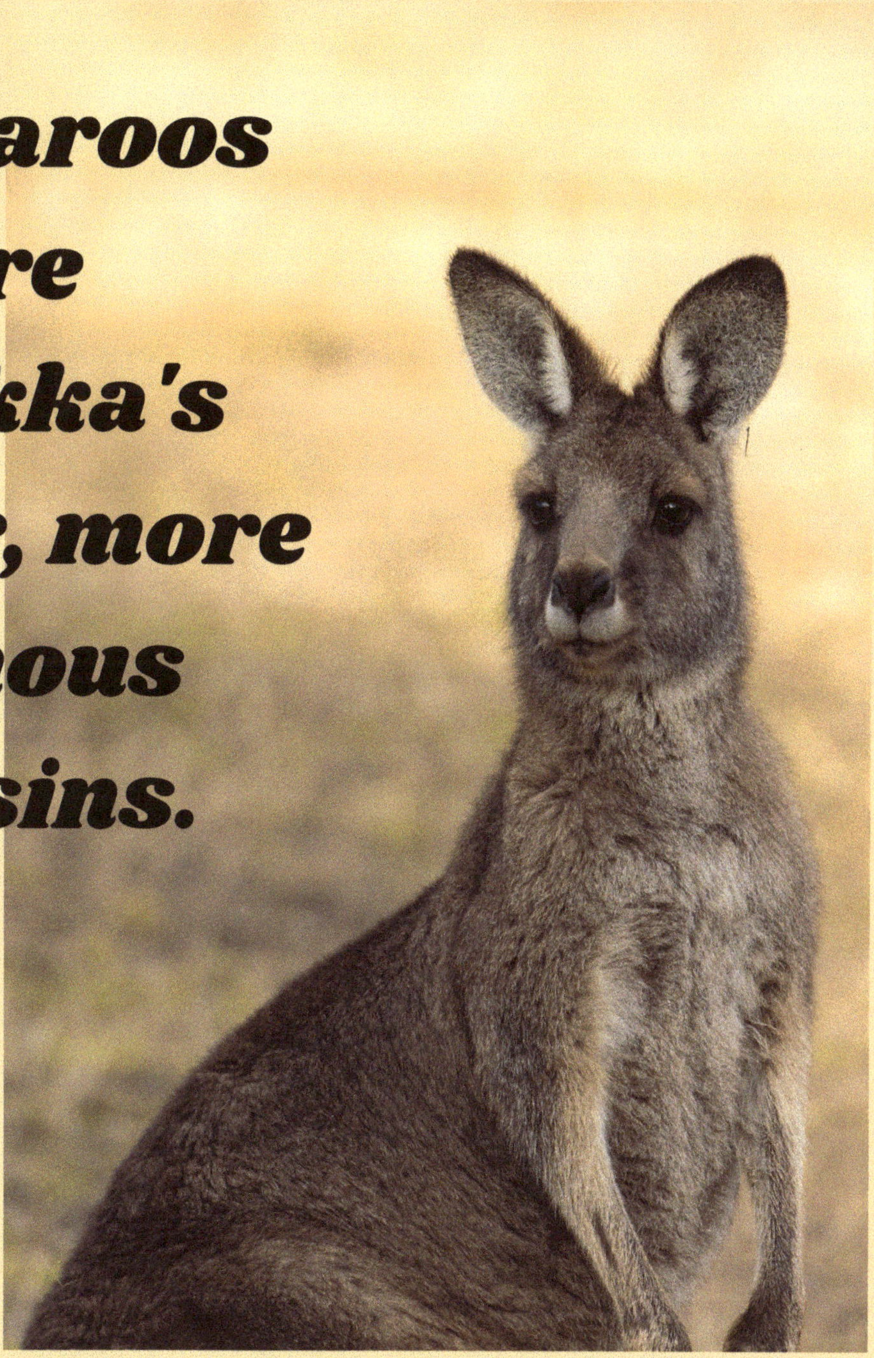

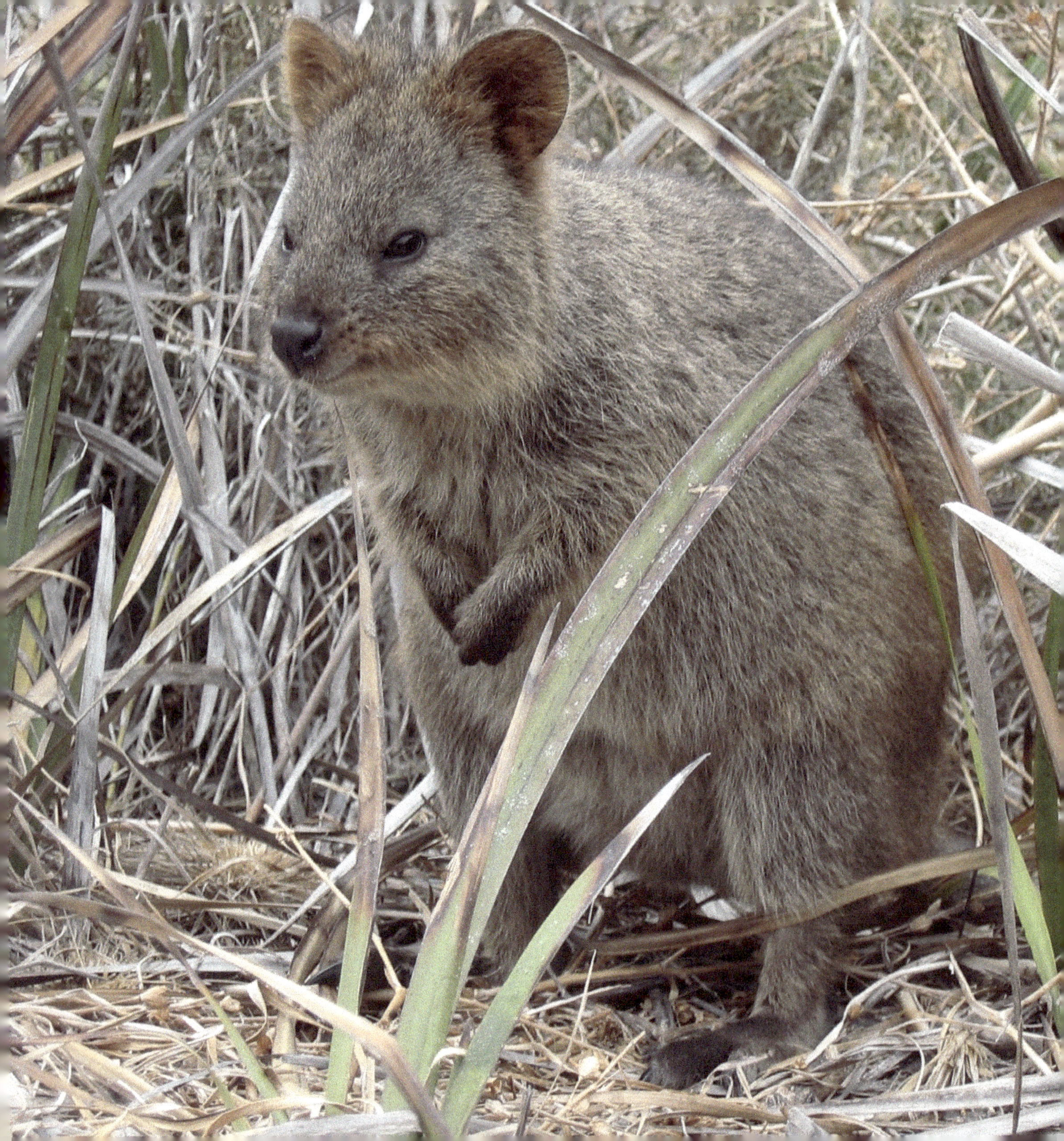

Quokka moms have pouches for their babies like kangaroos.

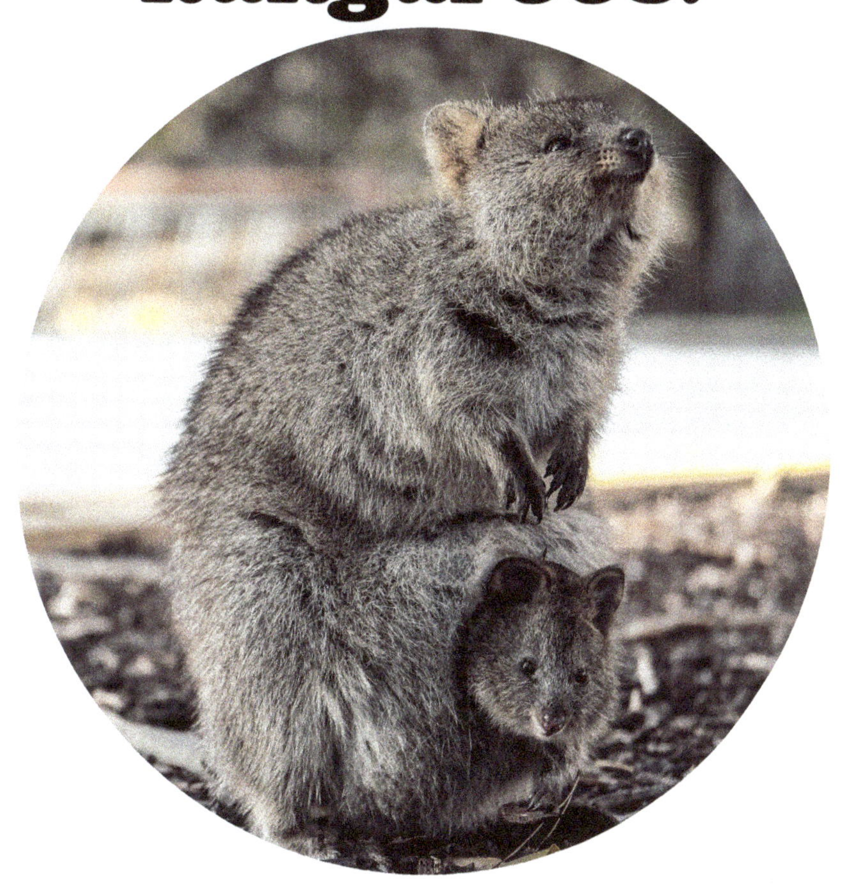

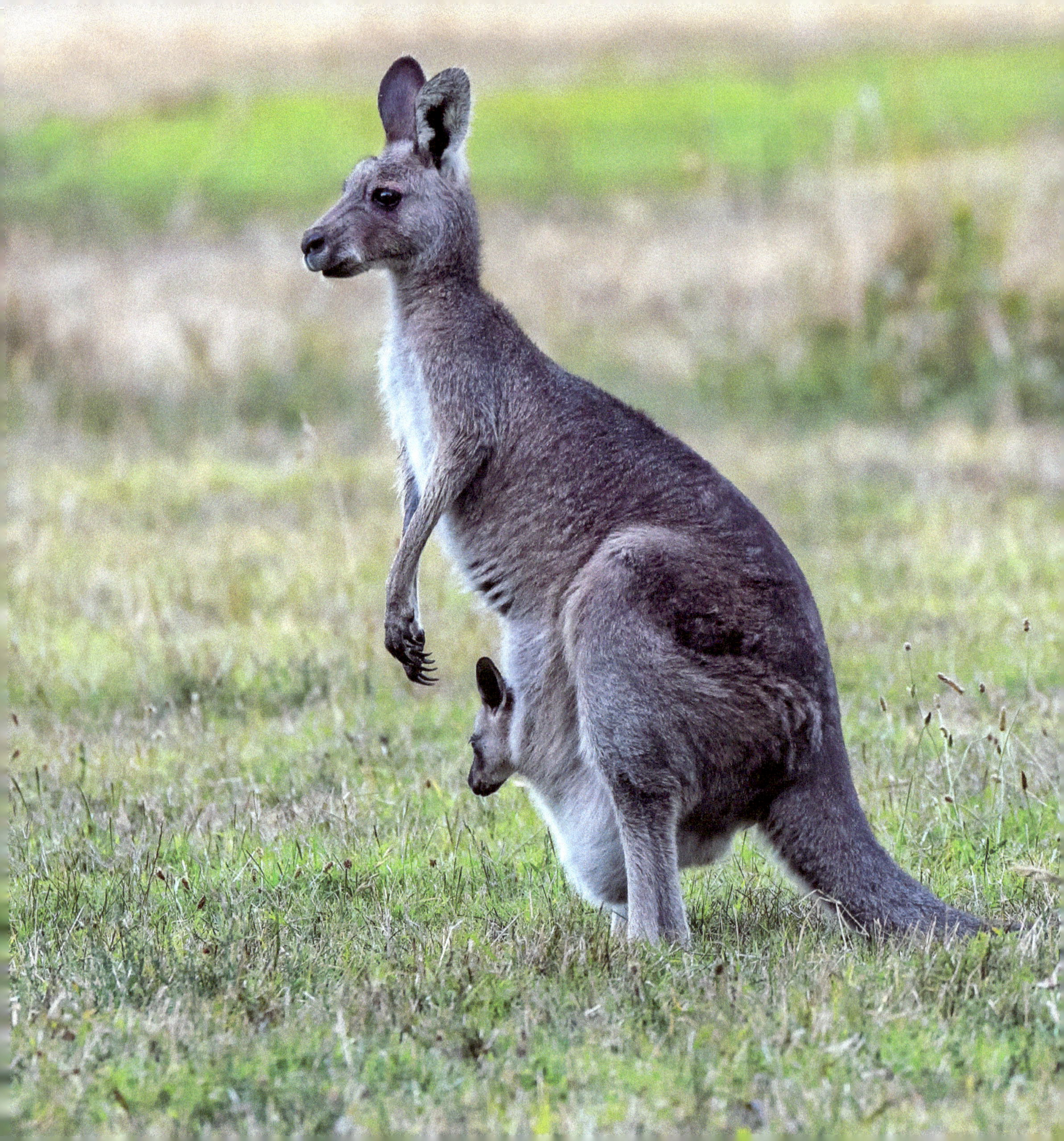

The Quokka babies
stay with their
mothers until they
are grown up.

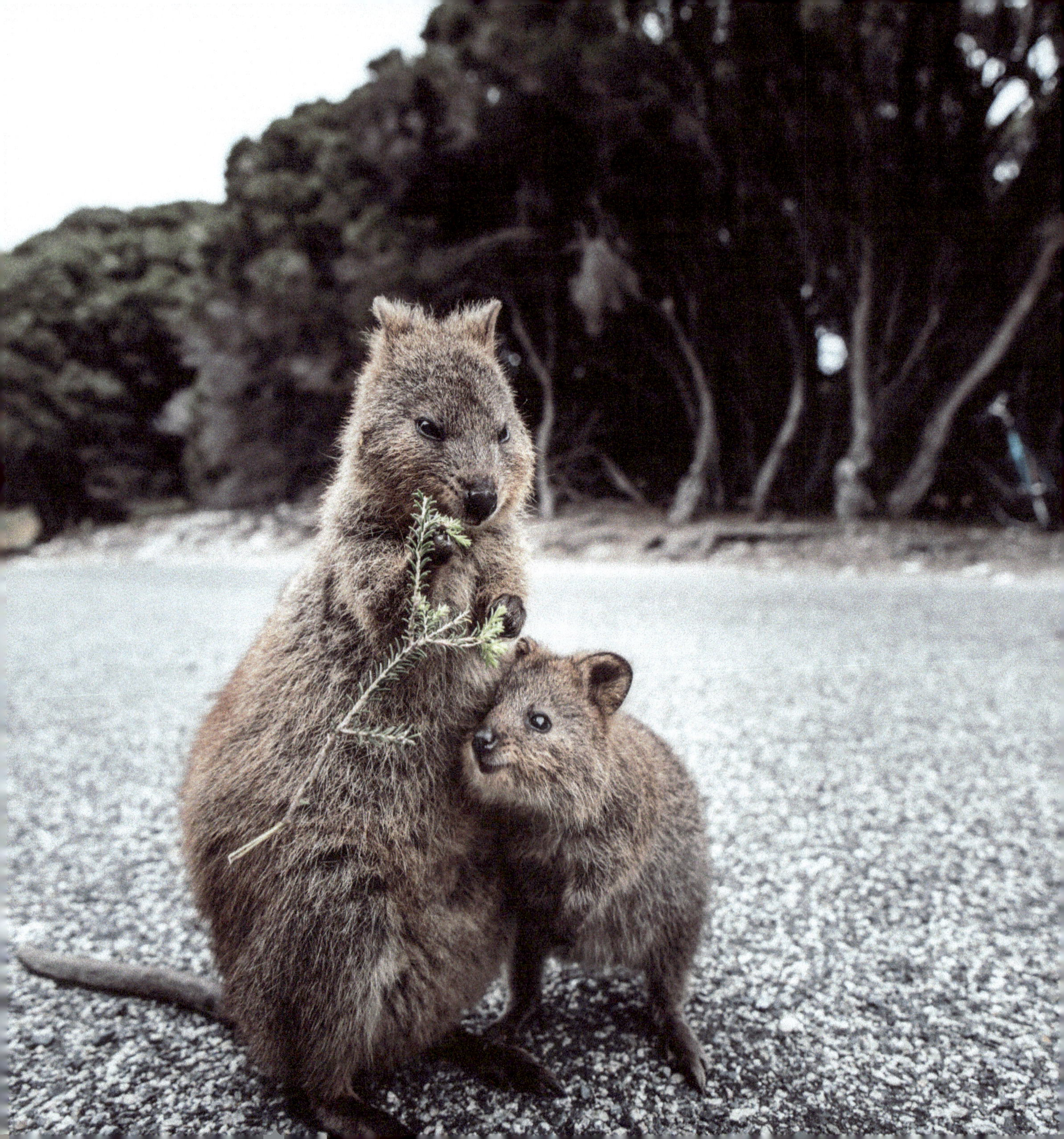

This Quokka mom is sharing her food with the child.

(Called a joey.)

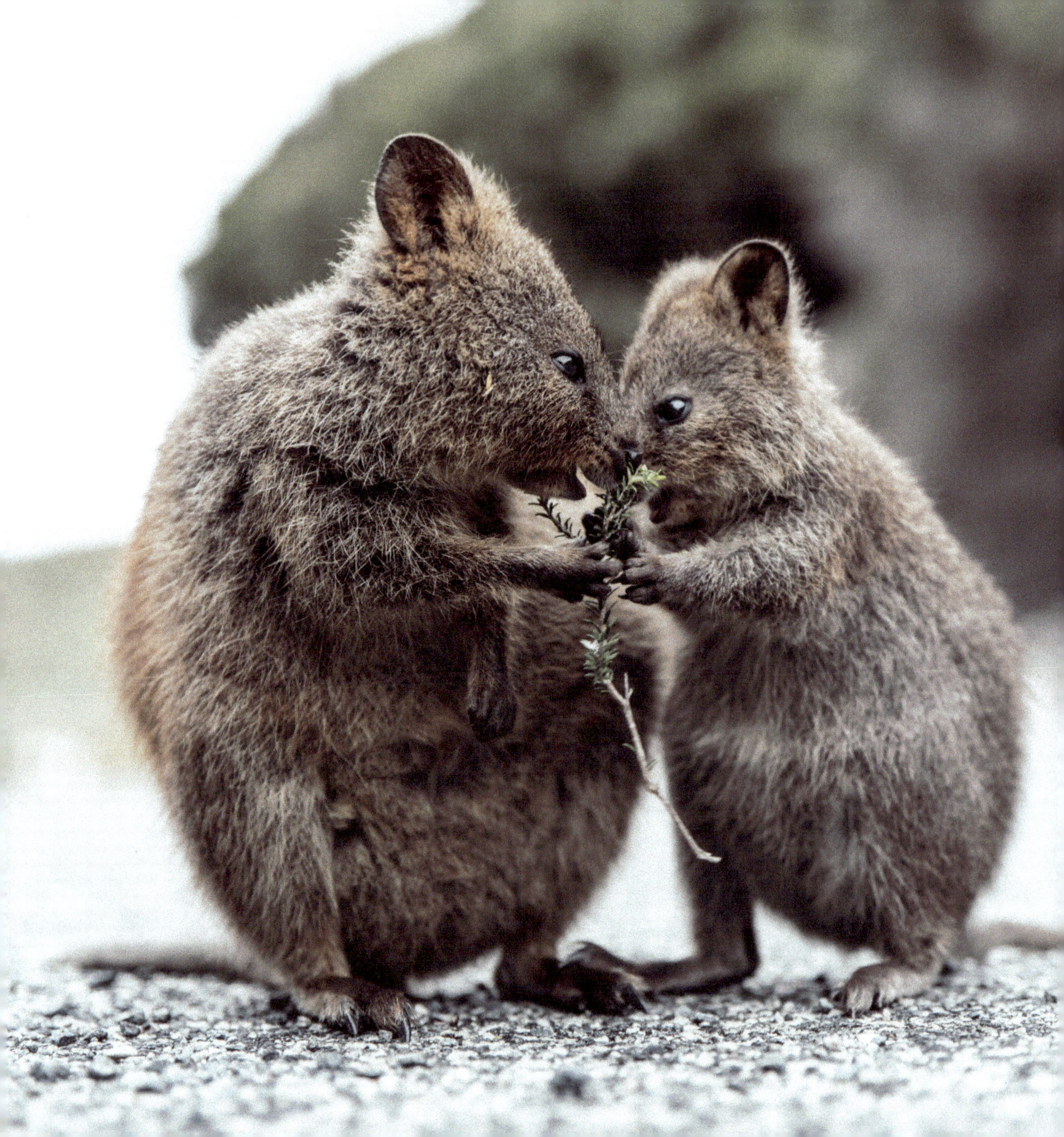

Quokkas have a happy smiling face & small round ears.

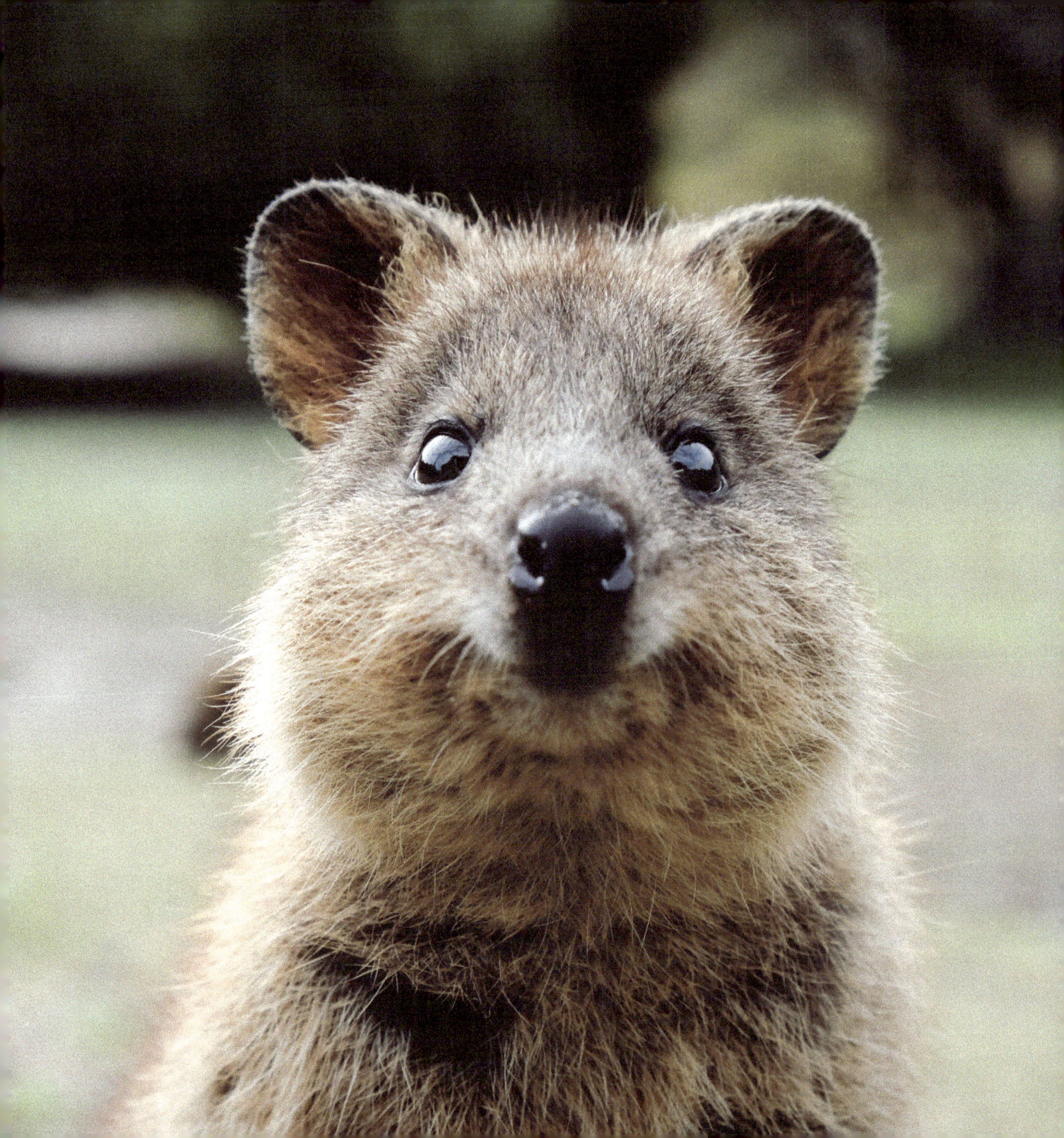

That smile brings lots of people to where most of them live.

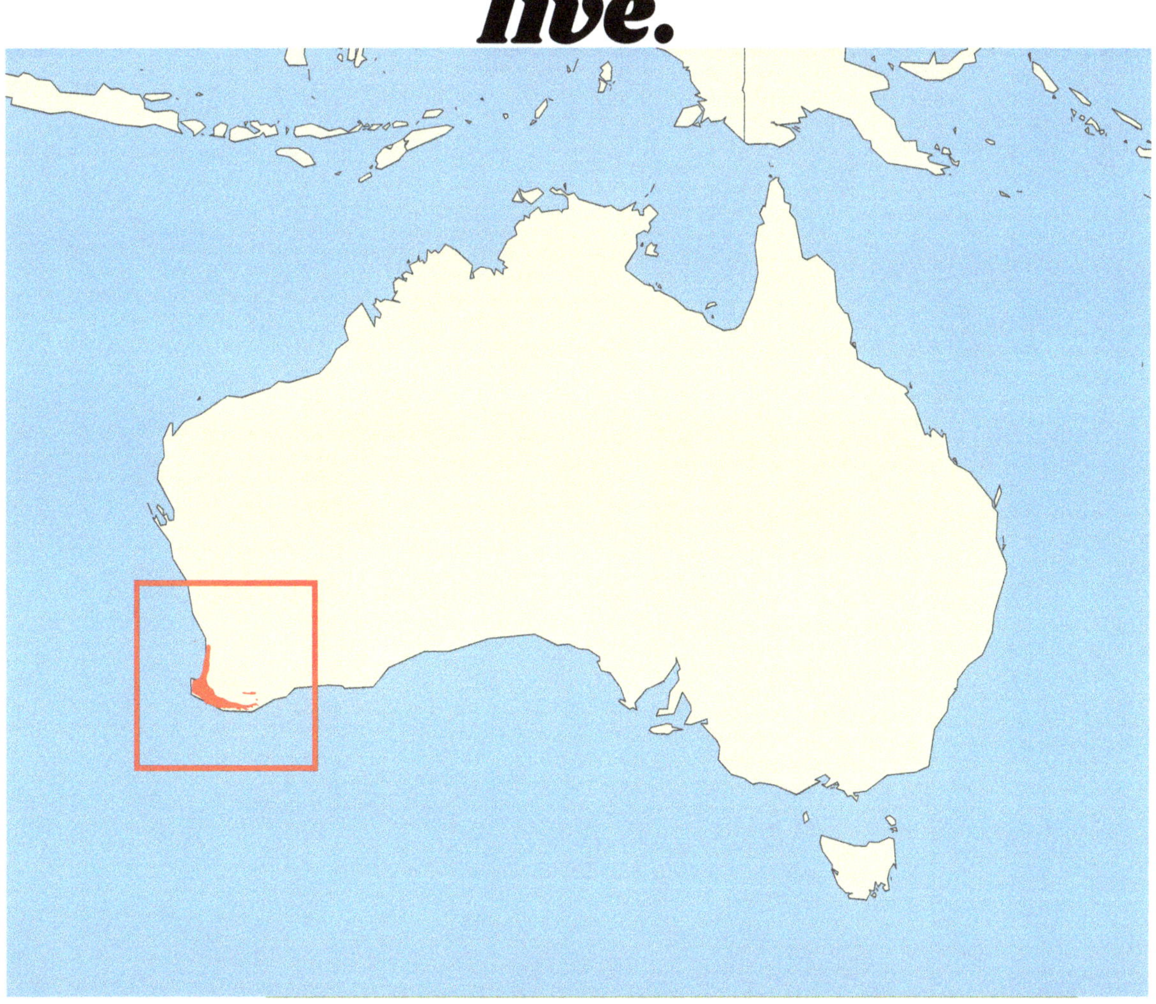

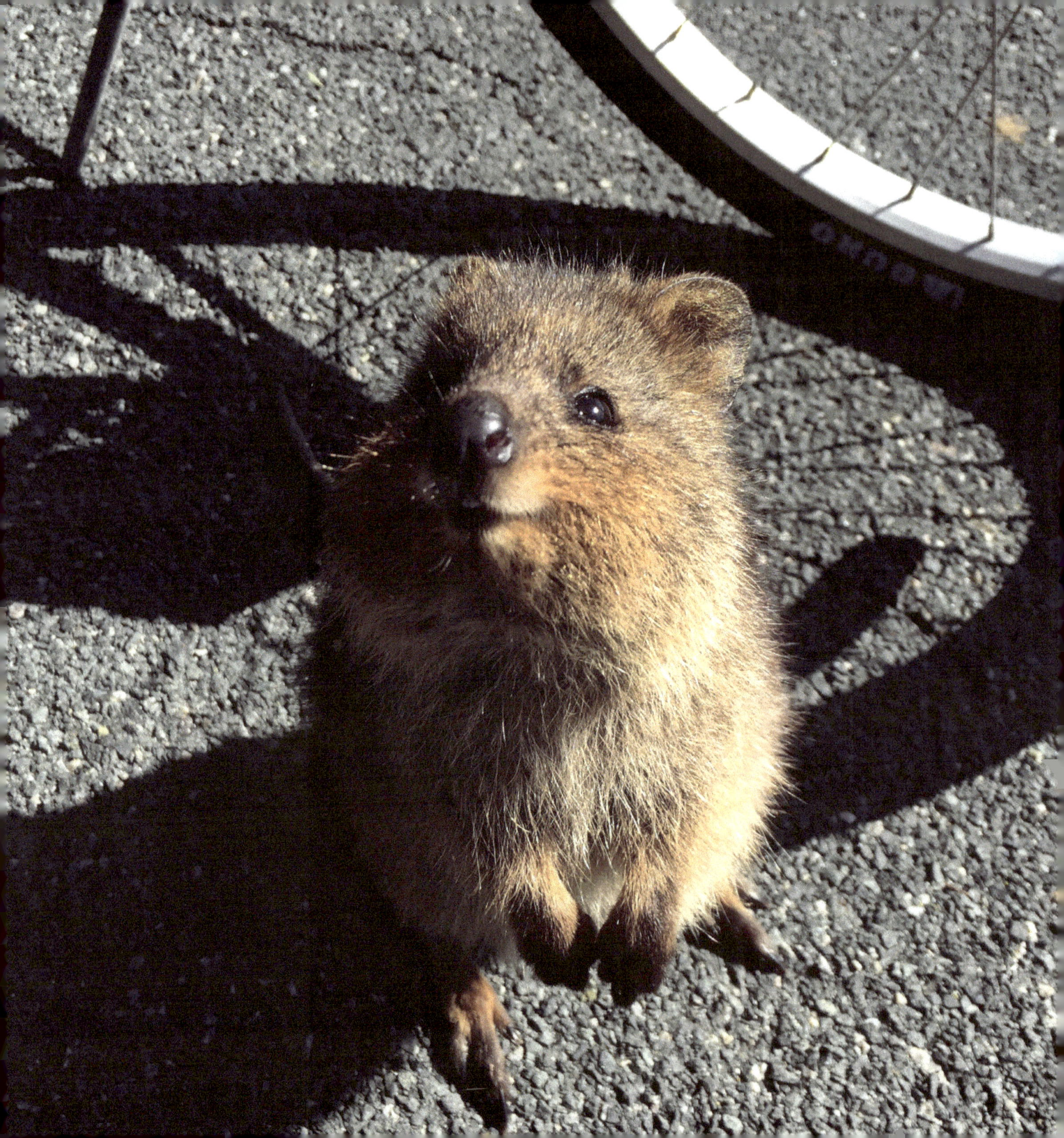

They spend some time
on the beach.

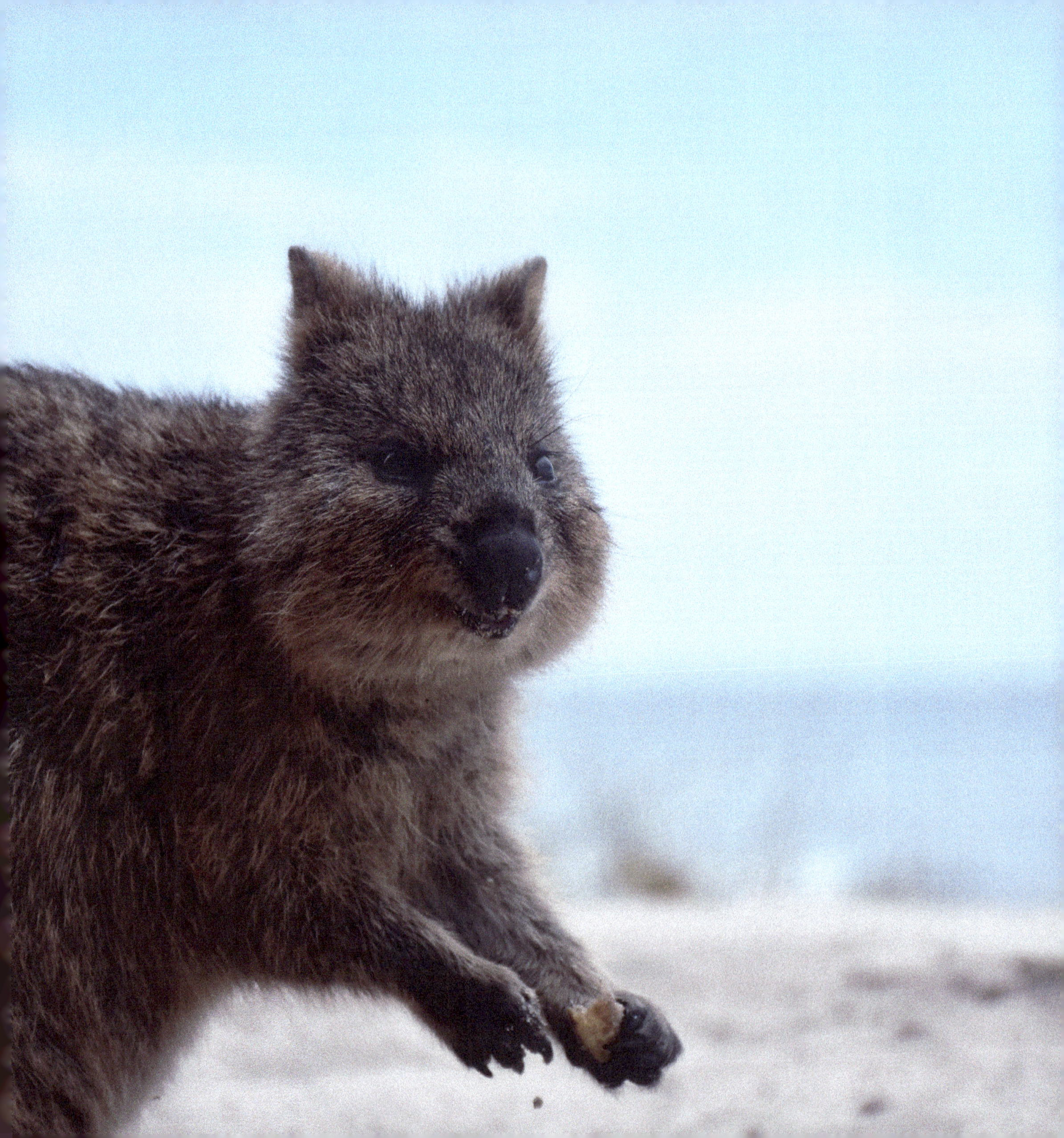

But most of the time they hide in grass or bushes.

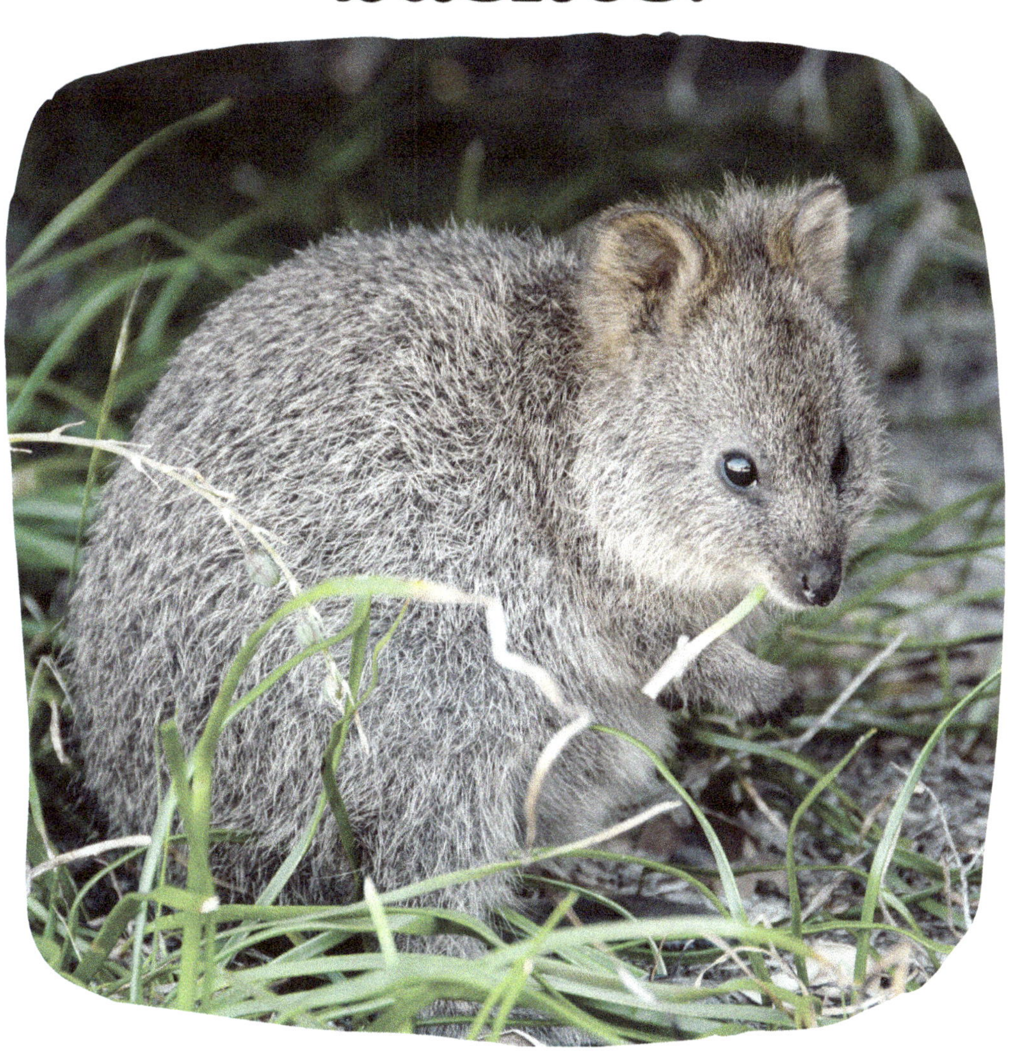

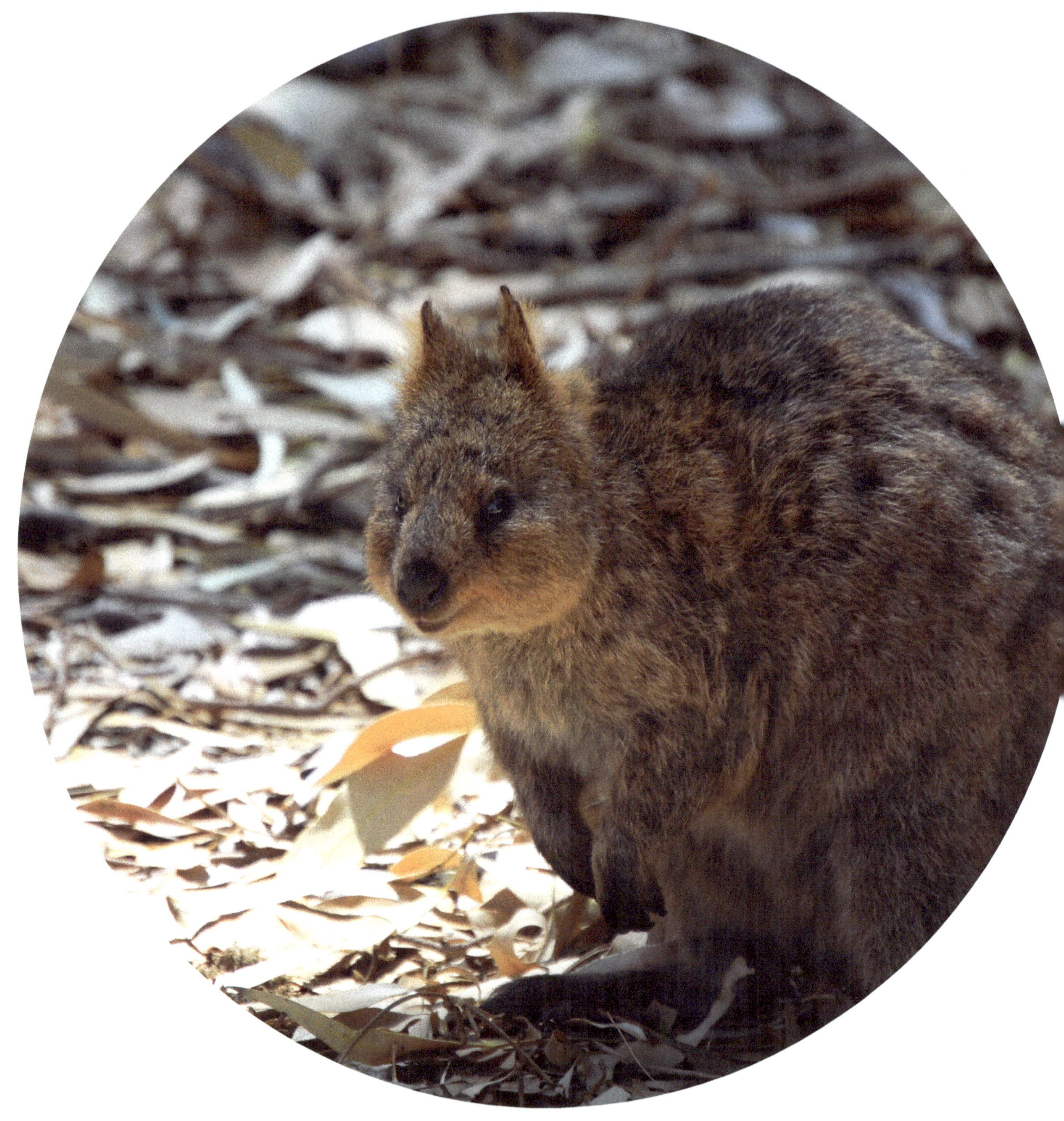

They find their food of grass, berries and leaves away from the beach.

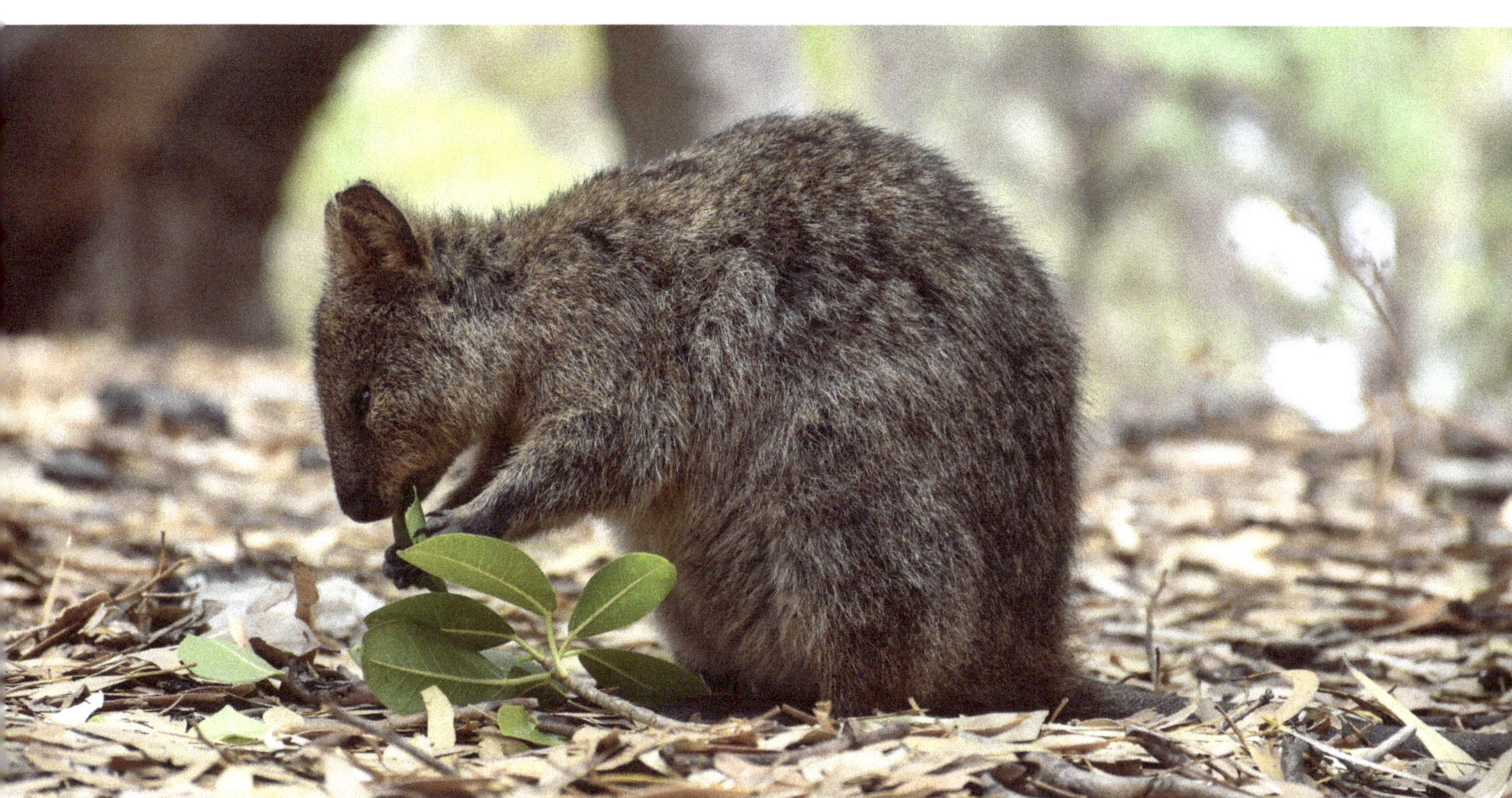

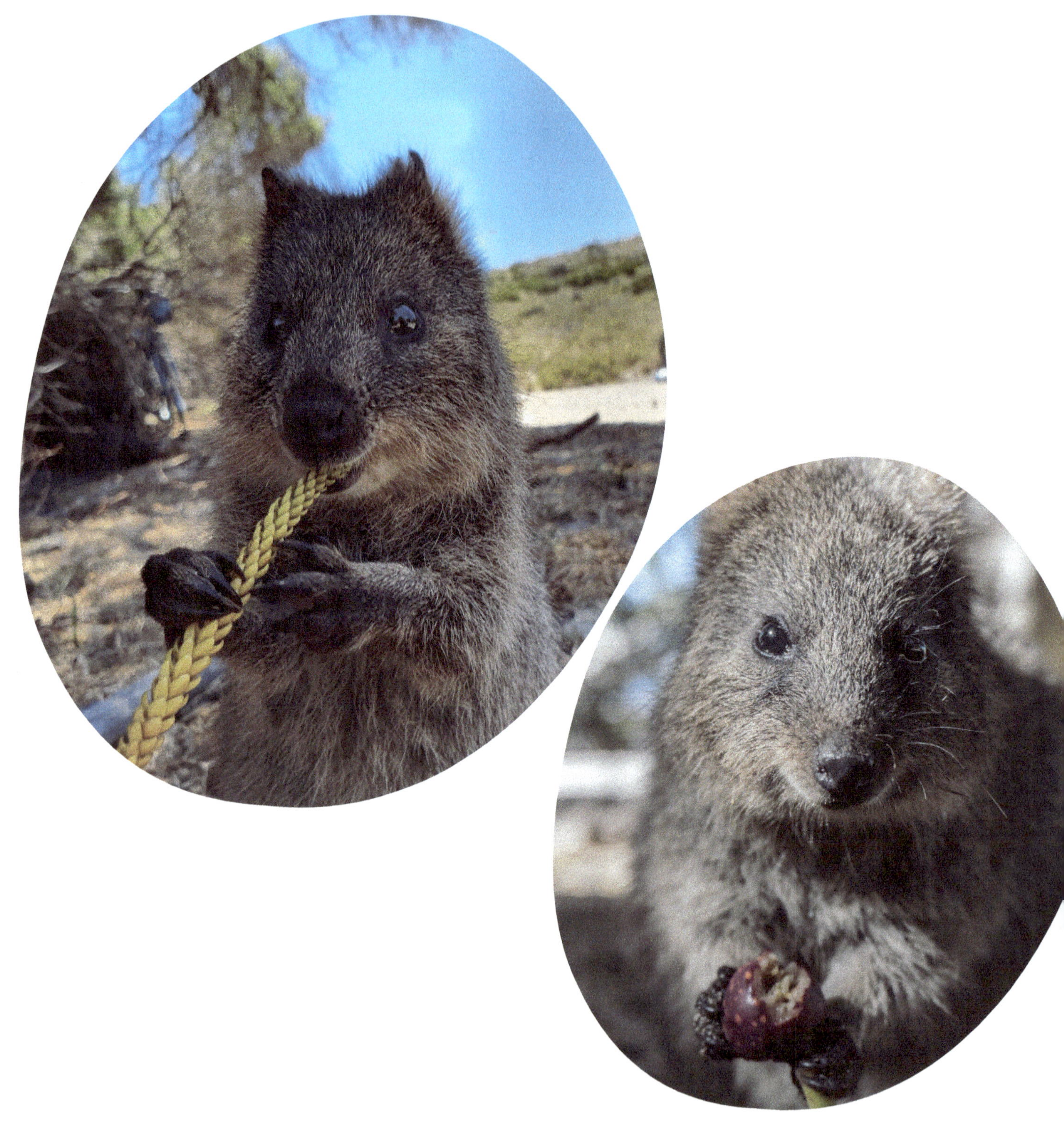

Quokkas spend most of their day napping. They are nocturnal, playing at night & sleeping in the day.

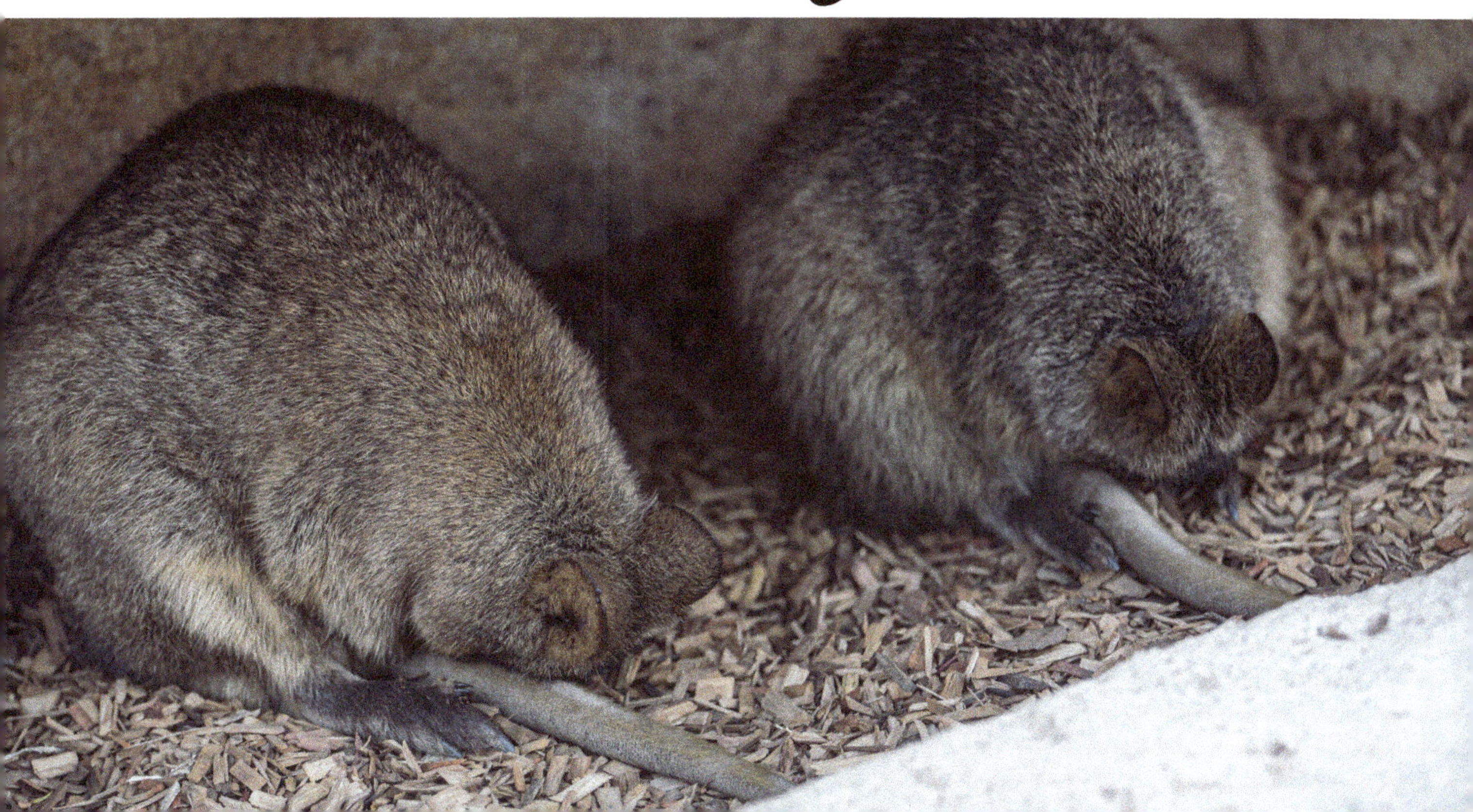

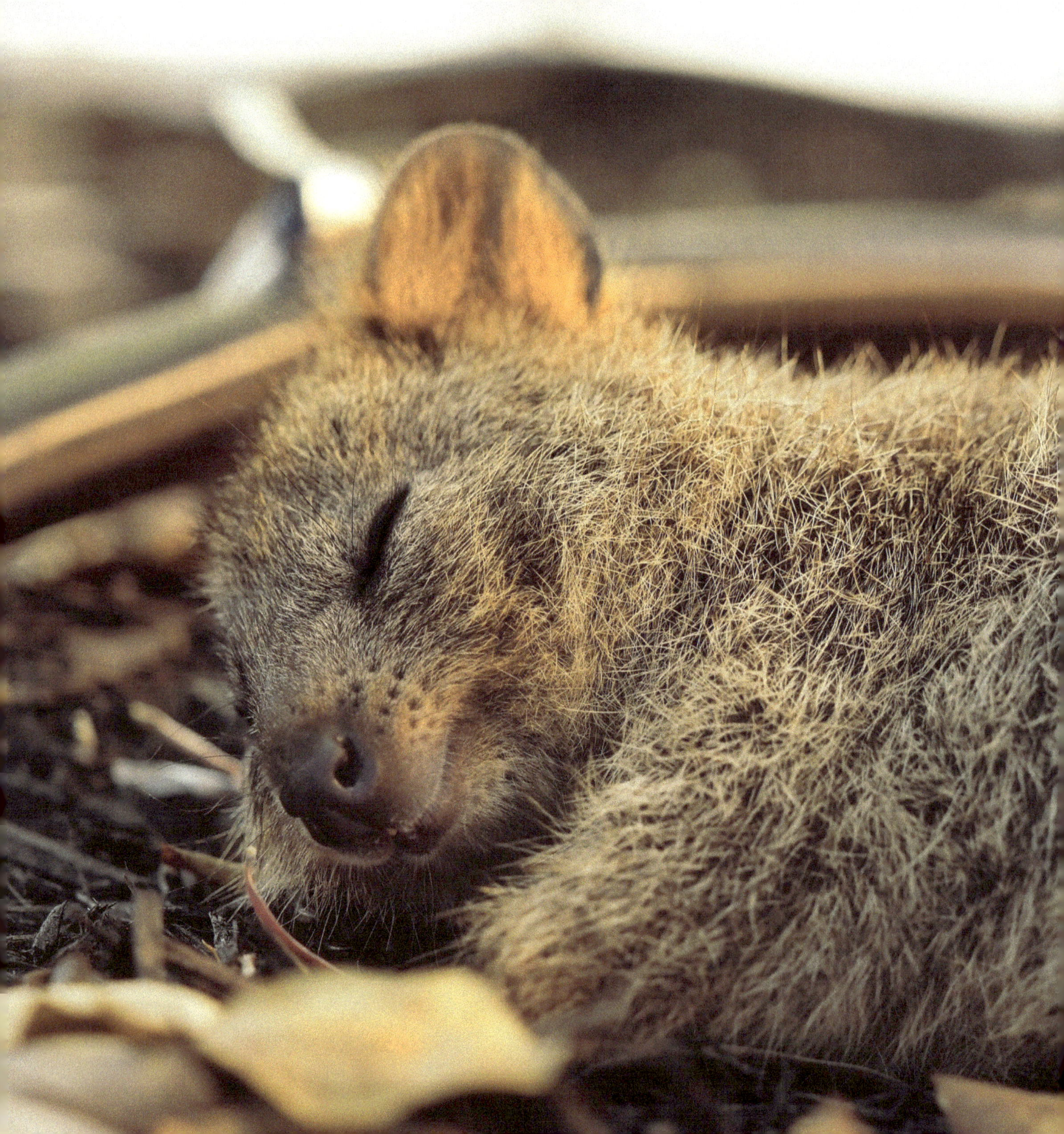

Quokkas may be small but the bring lots of joy into the world!

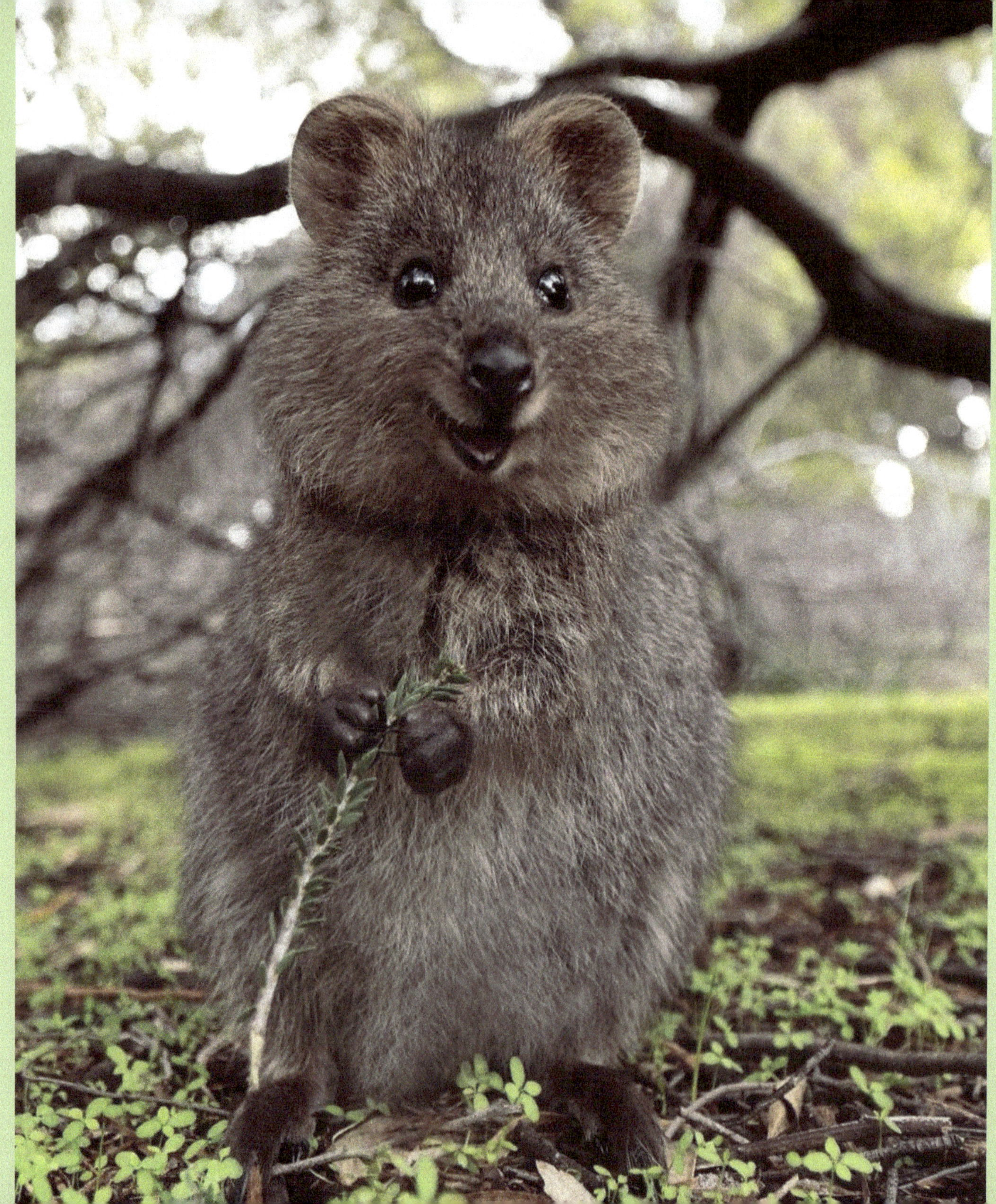

Quokka facts

Thank you for reading this early science book with your child. Please take a moment & write an honest review of it on Amazon to help other parents & teachers.

If you liked this book, check out our other books about animals:

My First Owl Book &
My First Shark Book.

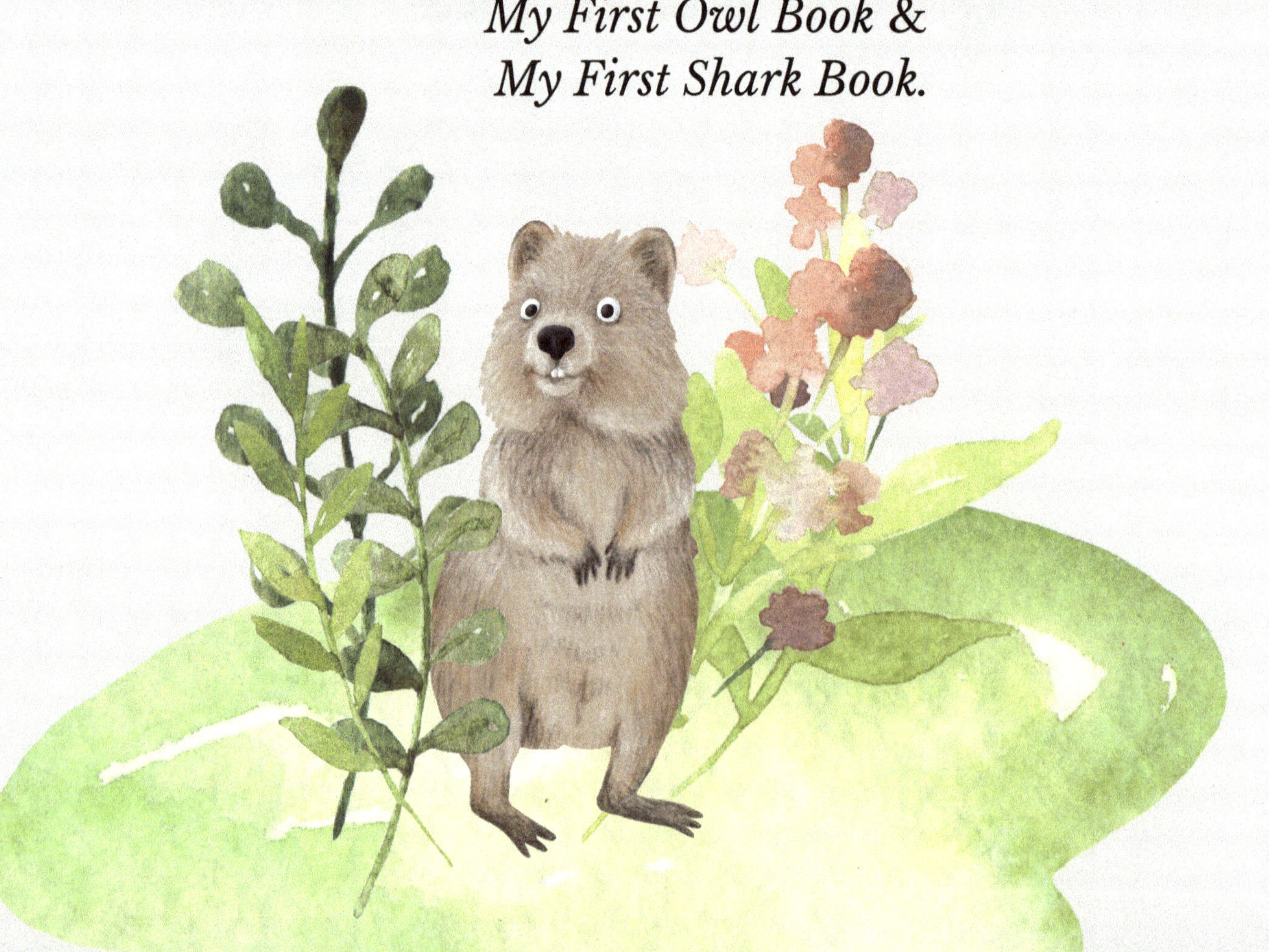